GEARED FOR GROWTH BIBLE STUDIES

FOCUS ON FAITH

A STUDY ON TEN OLD TESTAMENT CHARACTERS

BIBLE STUDIES TO IMPACT THE LIVES OF ORDINARY PEOPLE

Christian Focus Publications

The Word Worldwide

Written by Nina Drew and Stewart Dinnen

For details of our titles visit us on our website
www.christianfocus.com

ISBN 1-85792-890-3

Copyright © WEC International

Published in 2003 by
Christian Focus Publications, Geanies House,
Fearn, Ross-shire, IV20 1TW, Scotland
and
WEC International, Bulstrode, Oxford Road,
Gerrards Cross, Bucks, SL9 8SZ

Cover design by Alister MacInnes

Printed and bound by J W Arrowsmith, Bristol

CONTENTS

QUESTIONS AND NOTES

ANSWER GUIDE

PREFACE

GEARED FOR GROWTH

'Where there's LIFE there's GROWTH:
Where there's GROWTH there's LIFE.'

WHY GROW a study group?

Because as we study the Bible and share together we can

- learn to combat loneliness, depression, staleness, frustration, and other problems
- get to understand and love each other
- become responsive to the Holy Spirit's dealing and obedient to God's Word
  and that's GROWTH.

How do you GROW a study group?

- Just start by asking a friend to join you and then aim at expanding your group.
- Study the set portions daily (they are brief and easy: no catches).
- Meet once a week to discuss what you find.
- Befriend others, both Christians and non Christians, and work away together
  see how it GROWS!

WHEN you GROW ...

This will happen at school, at home, at work, at play, in your youth group, your student fellowship, women's meetings, mid-week meetings, churches and communities,

you'll be REACHING THROUGH TEACHING

INTRODUCTORY STUDY

The following studies are designed to focus our thoughts on FAITH, a concept with which we are all familiar – or are we?

Let's begin this Introductory Study by asking: 'What is faith?'

To help discussion consider these questions:

- In what ways do we need to exercise faith in daily living?
- What helps us to put faith into practice?

(As you pool ideas, your group leader might write them on a large sheet of paper.)

* * *

A story is told of six blind men who were asked to describe an elephant after being given a minute to 'get the feel' of it! One said an elephant was like a house (he'd felt its sides); one said it was like a tree (he'd gripped its leg); one said it was like a fat snake (he'd run his hands along its trunk). And so on.

Faith is like that. It has so many different aspects that it is a demanding task to compile a total definition. So, we are going to ask you to look at Hebrews chapter 11, which has been called 'God's gallery of faith – heroes', to discover the particular aspect of faith which each character contributes.

For instance, when we read about Abraham in verses 17-19 we learn that faith is obeying God even though it involves deep personal sacrifice and trusting Him implicitly about the final outcome.

As a group, discuss each character listed below and try to put in a sentence what you learn about FAITH from each one.

Verse	Character
4	Abel
5-6	Enoch
7	Noah
8-10	Abraham
11-12	Abraham
24-26	Moses
27-29	Moses
30	Joshua
31	Rahab
32-39	Gideon and Others

Now look at the definition of faith given to us in Hebrews 11:1 and 6. Would you say, from these verses, that faith is a combination of:

- putting absolute trust or confidence in God,
- being sensitive and obedient to His will; that means taking the next step He shows, even though we don't know the pathway ahead,
- living in a way that involves personal sacrifice because it cuts across worldly standards?

How do these 3 ideas tie up with what you have written on your sheet of paper? How does faith in God differ from faith in anyone or anything else?

* * *

Can you see faith operating at 3 different levels in the following testimonies?

1. David is a young married man with 2 small children. He writes:

> 'For four years I attended Church services and Bible Studies on a regular basis, seeking to know the truth about Jesus. I was trying to prove the claims of Jesus (e.g., John 14:6) before accepting them, but all I found were testimonies and statements from people supporting these claims. As I had been trained at University to be an Engineer, this sort of verbal argument was not the conclusive, tangible and logical proof I sought, but I could not gain peace of mind by dismissing the New Testament as being unfounded.
> 'In order to resolve this conflict, I gave up trying to prove Jesus, and just said I would believe. Now I, too, can testify that if you have faith in Jesus and ask Him into your life He is real, and answered prayer is all the proof anyone needs.'

2. 'One local church in Tasmania was challenged through a message given in Sunday morning worship about having a 'sense of direction' as far as its local strategy was concerned. The deacons conceded amongst themselves that there were indeed no 'unified, co-ordinated objectives towards which the congregation was heading.' So they decided to have an evening of prayer and discussion, waiting on the Lord for His Word to them as a fellowship. It came, with a unanimous conviction that a visitation campaign should be commenced in the vicinity of the church. Creative faith arose out of humbly acknowledging their lack of certainty and waiting upon God until the direction was unmistakably clear.'
   (Quoted from 'When I Say Move', S. R. Dinnen, CLC, UK, 1972)

3. Jenny says:

> 'As part of a team of Christian workers, my husband and I have seen overcoming faith vividly expressed in a young woman. After much prayer, holding on in faith for her and regular counsel, she wonderfully changed. Whereas before she was negative, rebellious and prone to ill health, she became free, positive and useful to the Lord.
> 'In the past 2 years she has worked as a nurse in some of the most difficult places in the world. This is nothing short of a miracle.'

The three levels suggested are:

1. *CLAIMING FAITH*
   This means simply accepting what God in His love graciously offers us, e.g., receiving Christ as Saviour (John 1:12).

2. *CREATIVE FAITH*
   This is a positive, expectant attitude towards God, believing that He will work in a specific situation; it will be accompanied by some practical step which commits the believer. For examples see Luke 5:1-8; 7:1-10; 8:43-48.

3. *CONQUERING FAITH*
   This is trusting God to overcome negative Satanic forces that are opposing or hindering His purpose, the basis of our faith being Christ's breaking of Satan's power at the Cross (1 John 3:8 and 5:4).

Can you fit the experiences of the characters in Hebrews 11 into one or other of these categories?

* * *

As we go on to study ten Old Testament characters who showed their faith by what they did, keep in mind the following words, and apply them to yourself day by day – 'Faith by itself, if it is not accompanied by action, is dead' (Jas. 2:17 NIV).

Are you in today's terminology, an 'Action Man' (or woman)?

Group members would benefit from reading biographies of people who have been strong in faith, e.g., Hudson Taylor, C. T. Studd, George Mueller.

STUDY 1
EVE – FAITH INTRODUCED

QUESTIONS

DAY 1 *Genesis 2:20-24.*
a) What reaction did Adam show to the wife whom God had created from Adam's own body?
b) What vital teaching on marriage can we learn from the way in which Eve was created (Eph. 5:33)?

DAY 2 *Genesis 3:1-6; 1 Timothy 2:14; James 1:13-15.*
a) Do you think Satan had some reason in choosing Eve rather than Adam to try his wiles on?
b) Matthew 4:1-11. Can you see some connection between the 3 areas of temptation Satan put to Eve and later to Jesus (compare Gen. 3:6 with Matt. 4:3, 6, 9)?
c) Suggest some illustrations of how we may be tempted along the same 3 lines.

DAY 3 *Matthew 4:4, 7, 10; Ephesians 6:16, 17.*
a) What are two powerful weapons against Satan's temptations?
b) Genesis 2:25 – Compare Genesis 3:7, 10, 21. What was the immediate effect of Adam and Eve's sin? Can we learn anything in our modern society from this?

DAY 4 *Genesis 3:8; (Ps. 139:7-12).*
a) What evidence do we have that sin breaks communion with God?
b) Romans 5:12, 18, 19. What far-reaching effect was there from the sin that Adam and Eve committed?

DAY 5 *Genesis 3:11-13 (compare David in 2 Sam. 12:13); Proverbs 28:13.*
a) What good things can we learn from their reply to God's challenge?
b) What bad thing should we avoid? (Compare Saul in 1 Sam. 15:19, 21.)

DAY 6 *Genesis 3:16; 1 Timothy 2:13,14.*
Comment on Eve's punishment.

DAY 7 *Genesis 4:1-16.*
a) Try to put yourself in Eve's place and describe how you feel as you hear about your firstborn Cain murdering his brother, and then being banished by God.
b) What are some lessons we can learn from the story of Eve's life?

NOTES

We commence this series of studies right at the beginning, with our first mother, Eve. God desired to have a whole family of sons and daughters who would love Him, and with whom He could have fellowship. As the home for this family, God created planet Earth, a tiny speck in the vastness of space. He began that great family with one couple, Adam and Eve, and planned that they should love and obey Him. He wanted them to depend solely on Him as the source of their life – physical and spiritual. That is what faith is all about.

EVE'S TEMPTATION – THE TEST AND FAILURE OF HER FAITH

We don't know how long Adam and Eve lived together in the Garden of Eden in perfect harmony with their Creator-Father God and with each other, enjoying complete fulfilment in their lives. Perhaps for many years. God could have made them mere puppets, but He preferred to have children who CHOSE to trust and obey Him. Hence the test. The Tree of the Knowledge of Good and Evil had been forbidden to them, since God planned that, as they lived in dependence on Him, He would guide them into all His will for them. He only had their welfare at heart.

Then, one day Satan the tempter, in the form of a wily serpent, came to Eve as she was alone near the forbidden tree. He began by putting doubts in her mind about the reliability of God's Word. Then came the insinuation that He was holding back something really desirable from her. The implicit faith Eve had always had in God's truthfulness and His love began to wane. The seeds of doubt took root. She gazed at the fruit, took it, ate it, and gave to her husband. He too, ate the fruit.

THE RESULT OF EVE'S FALL

Not only did Adam follow her example, but their children inherited a bent towards sin and independence. Death, physical and spiritual, for all mankind is the result of Adam and Eve's choice to act independently of God. And yet we see a spark of that old faith returning when, some time later, Eve exclaimed with joy, 'By the Lord's help I have acquired a son!' She never returned to that former perfection of faith, but she did recognize that she could not live her life apart from God. Have we recognized that fact?

GOD'S PROVISION FOR RESTORATION OF FAITH AND FELLOWSHIP

Although God had to expel His unfaithful children from the Garden of Eden, He did not desert them. He, Himself, made the first sacrifice for their sins, and clothed them with animal skins, a picture of the perfect sacrifice that Christ the Saviour would later make. And, lest we should think too harshly of Eve for giving us our fallen nature, God made a promise that through her would come the One who would deal a deathblow to Satan. Yes, Jesus was the offspring of mother Eve. In His sacrifice on the cross, Jesus undid all that Satan had done to the human race. And as we put our faith in Jesus, we become the sons and daughters God created us to be; those who would love and trust Him not because they have to, but because they choose to.

KEY THOUGHT: Faith is trusting God's Word, even when we do not understand.

STUDY 2
NOAH – FAITH RESPONSIVE AND REWARDED

QUESTIONS

DAY 1   *Genesis 6:5-7:1.*
a) Why was the Lord pleased with Noah?
b) What do you think his contemporaries thought of him?

DAY 2   *Genesis 7:1-12; Matthew 24:36-41.*
a) Of what New Testament idea is the ark a symbol or type?
b) What warning comes to this generation from the events of Noah's day?

DAY 3   *Genesis 7:13-24.*
a) What do you infer from the phrase 'the Lord shut them in'? (See also 2 Kgs. 4:1-7.)
b) What does the severity of the catastrophe tell us about the character of God?

DAY 4   *Genesis 8:1-22.*
a) Imagine the total ignorance of Noah and his family regarding their own future, the future of the ship, the future of the earth, and his inability to gauge the depth of the water. What then must the return of the dove with the olive leaf signify?
b) Compare Genesis 8:17 with Genesis 9:1, 7 to discover the common theme. How would you define 'spiritual fruit' (see John 15:16)?

DAY 5   *Genesis 9:1-7; 1 Peter 2:9.*
a) God gave Noah authority over the physical kingdom. In what sense does He give Christians authority in the spiritual kingdom?
b) Why do you think he included a prohibition on eating meat that still contained blood?

DAY 6   *Genesis 9:8-17.*
a) Spot the number of times the word 'covenant', 'agreement' or 'promise' occurs.
b) Could you state the content of God's covenant with Noah in one sentence of your own making?
c) What do you feel was the point of this covenant?

QUESTIONS (contd.)

DAY 7   *Genesis 9:18-28.*
a) What does this disappointing picture of Noah say to you?
b) Reviewing the whole episode and taking note of Hebrews 11:7 fill in
the blanks:
'Noah . . . God implicitly when He revealed the future and the impending
flood. Noah . . . God's instructions completely. The building of the ark
was a symbol of Noah's total . . . in God's word to him.'

NOTES

GET PAST THE SPECTACULAR TO THE SPIRITUAL!

Don't let the dramatic events of the Flood and the saving of the animals deflect you from the very rewarding study which you can make of the quality of Noah's spiritual life and of the Lord's dealings with him.

It was said of him that he 'walked with God' (Gen. 6:9); that he was without fault among his contemporaries whose lives had sunk to a very low level (Gen. 6:1-9, 11-13); that he publicly upheld God's standards (2 Pet. 2:5) although his efforts seem to have been rejected.

Imagine the abuse that must have been heaped upon him as worldlings viewed with amazement the construction of this huge vessel on dry land! If ever a Bible story was meant to encourage 'odd-man-out' Christians in a day of godless public standards, this is it!

WHAT IS A COVENANT?

Regarding the covenant with Noah, it is good to avoid the modern concept of an agreement or contract. In the Biblical covenants with Abraham, Moses, David, etc., it is GOD who takes the sole initiative out of Grace and out of Compassion for man in his need. It is not a bargain struck between two equal parties. The human party is enjoined by God to fulfil certain obligations, and God undertakes to fulfil His promises. For Noah, what was the obligation that God put upon him? (See Heb. 11:7.)

Christians are, of course, under the 'New Covenant'. Can you define the human obligation and the Divine promise? (See Heb. 10:16, 17.)

WAS THE FLOOD FOR REAL?

Many have queried whether the Flood ever took place, and if it did, what was the extent of it. Francis Schaeffer in 'Genesis in Space and Time' has this to say: 'It is interesting that among the common myths in the world's history, no other one is so widespread as the story of the Flood. From China to the American Indians ... one finds in strange forms the myth of the great Flood. Most of these myths have weird elements.... In the Bible, these strange and foolish elements are not there.'

THE FLOOD AND THE REST OF THE BIBLE

One cannot read the New Testament without getting the distinct impression that the Flood and the story of Noah are taken to be literal facts of history. The Lord Jesus used the experience of Noah and his generation to typify the attitude that would be prevalent when He comes again to the earth, Matthew 24:36-39. Isaiah records God as saying 'For this is as the waters of Noah unto me' when he describes God's assertion that He would act in mercy, Isaiah 54:9.

Another reference comes in 1 Peter 3:20 where it says that 'God waited patiently in the days of Noah, while the ark was being built.' Peter mentions the event again in his second letter when he warns scoffers that by the word of GOD 'the world of that time was deluged and destroyed' (2 Pet. 3:6). So, the Flood story is used to convey the message that the same certainty exists about the Second Coming. He uses the same event to assert the absolute inevitability of God's final judgment when he says 'He did not spare the ancient world when He brought the Flood on its ungodly people, but protected Noah, a preacher of righteousness' (2 Pet. 2:5).

KEY THOUGHT: The life of faith and obedience may result in some temporary derision, but it leads to permanent delight.

STUDY 3
SARAH AND HAGAR – FAITH BLOSSOMING
IN RECOGNITION OF GOD'S FAITHFULNESS

QUESTIONS

DAY 1 *Genesis 11:26-12:5.*
a) Where was Sarah's original home? Look it up on a map to gauge its approximate distance from Canaan.
b) What would Sarah's feelings be in leaving their home for a nomad's life?

DAY 2 *Genesis 12:10-20; 20:1-18 (note v. 12).*
What do you think would be Sarah's reaction to her husband's request that she should say she was Abraham's sister?

DAY 3 *Genesis 16; Proverbs 6:34; Song of Solomon 8:6.*
a) What was Sarah's motive in giving the Egyptian slave girl to Abraham as a second wife?
b) What was her motive in sending Hagar away on two occasions?

DAY 4 *Genesis 16.*
Hagar was originally an Egyptian slave girl (Genesis 16:1) who would be an idol-worshipper. What are some of the means God used to change her into a believer in the true God? (Note: the meaning of her son's name Ishmael is 'God hears'.)

DAY 5 *Genesis 17:15-18; 18:1-15; (Mark 9:24).*
a) It seems that both Abraham and Sarah had difficulty in believing God for a son in their old age. Yet Hebrews 11:11 commends their faith. Can we learn something about faith from this?
b) Can you think of any other women in the Bible who bore children contrary to nature?

DAY 6 a) Sarah called her son Isaac ('Laughter'). Contrast the laughter of Genesis 18:12 with that of Genesis 21:6.
b) What are some of the promises God had made to Abraham for Sarah's promised son (Gen. 13:15, 16; 15:4-6; 18:18; 22:17, 18)? Have these promises been fulfilled?

DAY 7 *Isaiah 51:2; Hebrews 11:11; 1 Peter 3:6.*
a) Why do you think Sarah comes into Abraham's story more than the wives of other great Bible characters?
b) Is there anything you particularly admire about this woman?

NOTES

SARAH

Two thousand years or more had passed since Eve made her tragic choice, and now we will look at another famous woman, Sarah. She lived with her husband, Abraham, in Ur the capital of the sophisticated, though idol-worshipping land of Babylon. This was the woman destined to be the mother of the nation of Israel, from which the Saviour would be born.

Let us try to imagine Sarah's conflicting emotions as her husband came to her with the announcement that God had told him to leave his country and kindred for a land that He would show them. Sarah had always loved and trusted her husband, and did not hesitate to accompany him. Abraham was later to be renowned for his faith (see Rom. 4), and we can be sure that Sarah's faith also grew as they faced the unknown together. And so the nomad life began. But Sarah was to discover that even a man of faith had his weaknesses. Abraham loved and admired his beautiful wife, and yet he could show cowardice and put his own safety before her welfare. Even though she suffered under such lapses, it seems she harboured no resentment towards him.

Oh, how she longed to satisfy the longings of his heart for a son and heir. Had not God promised that Abraham would be the father of many nations? And that all nations of the earth would be blessed through him? Perhaps she could help God out. So, swallowing her pride, she did what was the accepted practice of her time, and offered to him her slave girl, Hagar, as a concubine. Again, we see what influence women can have on their husbands. For, although Abraham would have been prepared to await God's timing, he agreed to Sarah's plan. Hagar soon became pregnant. If the Bible story had finished right there, we could probably write the sequel pretty accurately! On Hagar's part, pride and insubordination. On Sarah's, self reproach, unreasonable accusations against Abraham, and anger, spite and harshness towards Hagar.

Fourteen years passed. A further visit of the angel of the Lord to Abraham, with Sarah straining her ear at the tent door. 'Sarah your wife shall have a son.' Laughter, incredulity, yet doubt gradually gave place to faith. 'And the Lord did to Sarah as He had promised.' As the 90 year old mother nursed her son Isaac ('Laughter'), she exclaimed, 'God has made laughter for me.... I have born Abraham a son in his old age!' Even now her thoughts are on the joy she is bringing to her husband. And years later Isaiah was to say, 'Look to Abraham your father, and to Sarah who bore you.'

There is much we can learn as we look to this woman who, in spite of mistakes, is an example to us of love and faithfulness. Yes, she even won a place in the famous picture-gallery of heroes in Hebrews 11: 'By faith Sarah conceived ... for she considered Him faithful who had promised.'

HAGAR

How did this Egyptian slave girl feel as she was bought by an unknown foreigner to be the personal maid of his wife? How did she feel as she left her homeland and then as she found herself concubine to an 85 year old man? We do not know. But we do know that God loved this slave girl, rebellious and proud as she was, just as He loved Sarah, her mistress. On two occasions in her hour of great distress He appeared to her, and in great tenderness directed and encouraged her. And as He showed His love and care for her, faith in the one true God began to be born in her heart. No doubt the teachings and devotional life of Abraham had also impressed her greatly.

The birth of her son Ishmael had not been in God's perfect planning. Yet God assured Hagar of His care for her son. Ishmael was not the son of the covenant whom God had promised to Abraham. Yet God had a future for him also, as He does for each of us. Ishmael became the father of the Arab nations, a thorn in the flesh to the nation of Israel throughout the centuries, even to this day. God still overrules men's mistakes and looks upon us all as individuals. And so we find in Arab nations, as in all others, that God is calling out people for Himself, those who through faith in Jesus Christ have become our spiritual brothers and sisters. This can be an encouragement to us, for in spite of our own mistakes and the mistakes of others which may affect us, God still loves us and plans for us. Recognizing His great faithfulness encourages our faith to grow, as with Sarah and Hagar.

STUDY 4

CALEB – FAITH CONSISTENT, CONFIDENT
AND CONQUERING

QUESTIONS

DAY 1 *Numbers 13:1-3, 17-27.*
a) Why do you think God sent out this reconnaissance party? Do you see a principle relevant for us as Christians?
b) What significance was there in the type of men chosen?

DAY 2 *Numbers 13:27-33; 14:6-10.*
a) Pick out and contrast the statements of the ten and the two. What strikes you?
b) How do you account for the different conclusions reached?

DAY 3 *Numbers 14:11-24; 34-39.*
a) What does the dire punishment meted out to the spies and the nation teach us?
b) What was Caleb's secret? Try to express this in your own words.

DAY 4 *Deuteronomy 1:22-36.*
a) From this account what other insights do you gain about the reasons for Israel's failure at Kadesh?
b) What features about the character of God are apparent in this portion (see especially vv. 30, 31, 33)?

DAY 5 *Numbers 32:10-12; Joshua 14:6-14.*
a) What do you consider to be the outstanding quality of Caleb's life?
b) What strikes you as a good lesson for older people, in this passage?

DAY 6 *Reread Joshua 14:11,12, then read Joshua 15:13-19.*
a) From chapter 14:12 we might get the impression that Caleb was rather a demanding and grasping type. What saves us from this conclusion?
b) Chapter 14:12b and 15:14 show us Caleb still conquering his enemies. Specify any remaining spiritual 'foes' in your own personal life, that you need to overcome.

DAY 7 *Numbers 13:31-33; 14:1-4; Deuteronomy 1:27-30.*
a) 'No man is an island.' In what ways were people influenced by others in these passages.
b) Try to think of some people who have influenced your growth in the Lord. What made them useful? What can you learn from this?

NOTES

A REMARKABLE CHARACTER

Caleb was a great soul – courageous, tenacious and even pugnacious. His attitude of resolute confidence in the Lord makes this a fascinating study. His name is interesting. It means 'dog' – and if we conjure up the image of the British bulldog, we won't be far off the mark, because it would typify this robust, determined character who, along with Joshua, stands out in stark relief against the poor showing of his colleagues.

A ROUGH PROSPECT AHEAD

Let's back up a little and paint in a bit of the background. His story occurs during the period when Israel was on the move from Egypt to the promised land. God had led the nation out by a series of mighty miracles and they were now within striking distance of the area that was to become their home. But there were snags – the biggest being the attitude of the local inhabitants who, naturally, were prepared to give the invaders a rough time.

A RESPONSIBLE ATTITUDE

An operation was mounted to reconnoitre the target area. Twelve of the chief men – one from each tribe – were chosen to explore the country and to bring back a detailed report.

It is interesting to note that there was no disagreement on the FACTS which the twelve spies noted. The land was indeed fertile. (It took two men all their time to stagger home with one bunch of grapes slung between two poles!) But ten were full of consternation at the size and power of the opposition. What do you look at in times of crisis – the Opportunity or the Opposition?

Only Caleb and Joshua saw the Opportunity. What a difference ATTITUDE makes! Life situations in themselves do not determine our behaviour – it is WHAT WE THINK ABOUT THEM! On what is your evaluation mechanism based? Faith or Fear? The closer we are to the Lord the smaller our problems will appear, and the further away we are, the bigger they will seem.

A RESOLUTE FAITH

Caleb never wavers. He is the one who:
- urges the people to move in (Num. 13:30).
- asserts their capability for doing so (13:30).
- shows vexation at the nation's complaining attitude(14:6)
- draws attention to God's willingness to enable them (14:8).
- encourages a positive attitude (14:9).
- dismisses the enemy's strength as insignificant (14:9)

Note the numerous occasions in which Caleb's outstanding devotion and steadfast faith are mentioned:

Numbers 14:24	'He hath another spirit; he has followed me wholly.'
Numbers 32:12	'Caleb ... and Joshua ... have wholly followed the Lord.'

Deuteronomy 1:36	'He has wholly followed the Lord.'
Joshua 14:8	'I wholly followed the Lord.'
Joshua 14:9	'The land ... shall be thine inheritance ... because thou hast wholly followed the Lord.'
Joshua 14:14	'He wholly followed the Lord.'

Almost his last words indicate his total reliance on the word of the Lord. 'Give me this mountain.... If the Lord is with me, then shall I be able to drive them out, AS THE LORD SAID' (Josh. 14:12).

KEY THOUGHT: Your testimony of Faith will certainly CONTRAST with the unbelievers; may it also CONVICT and perhaps even CONVERT!

STUDY 5

REBEKAH – FAITH DIMINISHING THROUGH SELFWILL

QUESTIONS

DAY 1 *Genesis 24:1-4,10-20.*
a) Describe the young woman, Rebekah.
b) How was Rebekah related to Abraham?

DAY 2 *Genesis 24:50-58; Psalm 127:3.*
a) In the natural it would seem very risky to go off with a complete stranger to marry a man she had never met. What do you think reassured Rebekah that all would be well?
b) Comment on the blessing that Rebekah's family gave her (v. 60). How was this blessing fulfilled (Gen. 28:13, 14)?

DAY 3 *Genesis 24:61-67.*
a) What do you think the conversation of Rebekah and the servant would have been during the long journey to Canaan?
b) Their marriage started happily (v. 67). What are some of the contributing factors to this?

DAY 4 *Genesis 25:20-26.*
a) What does this passage tell us of the faith of Isaac and Rebekah? How long after their marriage had they waited for the birth of their children?
b) Genesis 25:27, 28 (see Gen. 37:3, 4). The birth of children should draw a couple closer together. Why did it not in this case? What is there for us to learn here?
c) We are told why Isaac loved Esau. Why do you think Rebekah loved Jacob more? For what reasons can we be tempted to love one child more than another?

DAY 5 *Genesis 26:6-11 (Gen. 12:13).*
What would Rebekah feel about the cowardice Isaac shows here?

DAY 6 *Genesis 27:1-29.*
a) Rebekah would probably justify her scheming on the grounds of God's statement of Genesis 25:23. Comment on this. Can you quote the case of another woman who schemed to bring God's promises to pass with disastrous results (remember Study 3)?
b) Can we sometimes be guilty of the same thing? How?

QUESTIONS (contd.)

DAY 7 *Genesis 27:30-45.*
a) Rebekah's strategy was successful, yet it brought tragic results. What were some of these?
b) What were the strengths and weaknesses of Rebekah?

NOTES

We turn today to look at a woman whose marriage started with great promise, yet later turned sour. We all know friends whose experience has been like Rebekah's. Perhaps you need look no further than your own home. However, we know that broken relationships do not have to remain that way, and Jesus specializes in teaching us how we can mend them.

REBEKAH'S MARRIAGE – LOVE DEVELOPING

Strange as it may seem to our western minds, it was not Isaac who took the long journey to woo for himself a bride, but his faithful, godly servant. As Rebekah fulfilled everything that this man had asked of God, she and her family knew that God had chosen her to be the wife of the princely Isaac. When God plans a marriage everything is set for a life of love and contentment. Our part is to put our trust in Him and in the partner He has provided, and together allow God to be the head of our home.

There was real love from the start in their married life; love for each other and for God. They lacked nothing in material goods. Only one unfulfilled need remained. A child would complete their happiness. They were a couple who had faith, so they prayed to God and He answered their prayer. Surely now their cup of happiness would be full.

What excitement there must have been during her pregnancy when God explained to her the meaning of all that energy that was going on inside her. She was going to have twins! What joy when the labour was over and two beautiful babies lay beside her. Rebekah's life was very full. How fortunate she was to have maid servants and her gentle Isaac to help. Surely, now their marriage would know true fulfilment.

REBEKAH'S MARRIAGE – LOVE DIMINISHING

But the very event that had brought such joy was soon to be the cause of friction. In Isaac's eyes, Esau could do no wrong. In Rebekah's, he could do nothing right. Communication between husband and wife seems to have broken down. We saw from the start that Rebekah was a strong-minded woman with initiative and energy. But, as time went on, that natural drive that could be such a creative force was used in a purely negative way. God had told her that Jacob would be the head, not Esau the firstborn. Yet, rather than let God work it out His way, Rebekah was determined to bring it about herself. She would stop at nothing in order to see her favourite son promoted to the privilege of firstborn. No matter if her ageing husband, now blind and bedridden, was deceived and deeply hurt. No matter if Esau was to cry out in an agony of despair. Rebekah must get her own way.

The woman who once had trusted God and loved and respected her husband, stooped to a despicable trick. And when Jacob hesitated to comply, fearing that his father's blessing might be turned into a curse. Rebekah had retorted, 'On me be your curse, my son!' And so it turned out. The result was further estrangement from the husband and son she had come to despise, and even the son she doted on was forced to flee for his life. Rebekah never saw him again. And could it be that Jacob was relieved to get away from the mother who had manipulated him right up to manhood? We pity Rebekah. Perhaps she later repented; the records are silent.

THE CAUSE OF THEIR MARRIAGE BREAKDOWN

The main cause must surely have been Rebekah's failure to trust God to work out His purposes in her family. And with that came self-will, a determination to work things out her way. Love and respect for her husband could no longer exist in that climate. Both partners were at fault in showing favouritism in their family, resulting in estrangement and a total breakdown in communication.

Perhaps we see some of Rebekah's unfortunate traits in our own lives, whether we be married or single. Perhaps those traits have caused tension in our family, social, church or business lives. But, if we admit where we have been wrong and ask Jesus to come into our family and personal lives in a new way, He will begin to work in us and in our situations, healing relationships and making us the people He wants us to be.

KEY THOUGHT: Diminishing faith produces hardness and lack of love.

STUDY 6
GIDEON – FAITH OVERCOMING FEAR

QUESTIONS

DAY 1 *Judges 6:1-13.*
a) What was the lesson that God was seeking to teach Israel through its history?
b) What mistake did Gideon make in his response to the Lord?

DAY 2 *Judges 6:14-27.*
a) What second mistake did Gideon make?
b) What message did the Lord have to repeat for Gideon's sake?

DAY 3 *Judges 6:28-40.*
a) He was obviously a fearful person (see vv. 15, 23, 27 and 7:10, 11). The Lord encouraged his faith by giving the signs he asked for (6:36-40). Should we adopt a similar course of action?
b) It says in verse 34 that 'the Spirit of the Lord came upon Gideon.' What were the results?

DAY 4 *Judges 7:1-14.*
a) What would the reduction of the size of Gideon's task-force do for him?
b) What did the visit to the Midianite camp do for him?

DAY 5 *Judges 7:15-25.*
a) What is the proof that Gideon's faith had reached its peak?
b) What would have been the effect of Gideon's strategy in the minds of the Midianites?
c) As a soldier of the Lord, do you have a sense of God's goals for you? And a strategy for reaching them?

DAY 6 *Judges 8:1-17.*
a) What evidences are there that Gideon had the qualities of a good leader?
b) How do we know that Gideon's confidence was remaining strong?

DAY 7 *Judges 8:18-35.*
a) For all the good that Gideon achieved under the Hand of the Lord, Israel's renewal seems to have been short-lived. Could Gideon be blamed for this?
b) What actual mistake or mistakes do you feel he made, latterly?

NOTES

THE MERRY-GO-ROUND

The story of Judges is God's merry-go-round. Except that we would really have to call it a 'misery-go-round'. A distinct cycle of events recurs in this book (which, by the way, covers the early period of Israel's settlement in the promised land). The days of strong leadership under Moses and Joshua were over. The nation lacked a central administration, and the era of the prophets – who brought directive messages to the nation from the Lord – had not yet begun. People just pleased themselves.

This is where the misery-go-round comes in. When materialism and self-indulgence reigned and the worship of God diminished, the inevitable happened – tough times came to the people. The displeasure of the Lord and His means of bringing the people back to Himself, were in the form of invasion from neighbouring powers. When there was a resurgence of spiritual concern and a repentant cry for deliverance, He would raise up 'judges' or deliverers – men strong in faith and physique – who, under His anointing would lead the people, rid the land of invaders and reconstitute a pattern of God-centred living and worship throughout the land. Such was Gideon.

THE MORASS

As the personal influence of these deliverers waned, the people slid back into spiritual indifference and self-pleasing, with the result that God would again allow them to come under the heel of a foreign oppressor. So the cycle would repeat itself.

THE METAMORPHOSIS IN GIDEON

Gideon could be called God's chicken-hearted hero. Time after time one can sense that his knees are wobbling and his mind is dithering. Yet, with all his human limitations, he comes through in crisis after crisis with the word and the act of faith which marks him out as a true leader, totally dependent on the Lord's sufficiency. So, there's a great lesson for us in this story.

The opening scene is typical. He is down in a pit usually kept for crushing grapes, threshing wheat because he doesn't want to be seen by the marauding Midianites who would have swooped down and relieved him of his precious harvest.

And then, when the angel of the Lord calls him, he says his family is poor and he's the least important member of it!

MIRACLE AT MEALTIME

And as for needing continual signs and reassurances, Gideon surely takes the cake. Although in one instance an angel took the cake. In Chapter 6, he makes a meal for this angel in the hope that he will give him some indication that his message from the Lord is authentic. Poof! In a trice the cakes and meat are consumed by miraculous fire.

Later, he has to have more signs that the Lord is with him. So, he asks that a fleece left out overnight will be covered with dew and the earth round about be dry. It happens – but he's still not convinced, so he reverses the request the next night!

In chapter 7 he has to have a sign that Israel is going to defeat the Midianites in a forthcoming battle and the Lord provides for this too, by giving him an insight into what the Midianites are thinking. What a woeful waverer – but God turns him into a wonderful winner!

THE MESSAGE OF GIDEON
His leadership did not rest upon public demand, personal desires or pride in his abilities. It was entirely based upon the call of God, the conviction that God was with him, courage that came from absolute faith in the Lord's resources, and the 'clothing' of the Holy Spirit.

KEY THOUGHT: The glory of faith is the possibility of unbelief. 'Light' has no meaning unless there is darkness. To be assaulted by feelings of unbelief is not sinful; to refuse to believe is.

STUDY 7

RACHEL AND LEAH –
FAITH TRIUMPHING IN DIFFICULT CIRCUMSTANCES

QUESTIONS

DAY 1   *Genesis 29:4-20.*
a) It seems the village well was quite a social gathering place. Can you think of other romances that started at a well? (You can find one in Gen. 24 and another in Exod 2.)
b) How do we know that Rachel and Jacob's attachment was really a 'love match'?
c) What do you feel are the main ingredients in a good marriage?

DAY 2   *Genesis 29:21-25.*
a) What do you think about Leah's part in her father's deception of Jacob?
b) How would this incident affect her relationship with Rachel?

DAY 3   *Genesis 29:31-35; 30:2; (1 Sam. 1:27, 28).*
a) How did God comfort Leah in the rejection she was feeling?
b) Discuss the verse, 'Children are a heritage from the Lord' (Ps. 127:3), and the responsibilities this verse implies.

DAY 4   *Genesis 30:1-8.*
a) What plan did Rachel devise to get equal with her sister?
b) Who else carried out the same plan, from a different motive (Gen. 16:2)?
c) Which verses of Genesis 30:1-8 show us that Rachel still has much resentment towards her sister? (Discuss Heb. 12:15.)

DAY 5   *Genesis 29:30-34; 30:1; (Heb. 12:7-11).*
a) What was the biggest heartache Leah carried through her married life?
b) And the biggest heartache Rachel carried through the early years of her marriage?
c) Apart from marriage difficulties, suggest some similar trials that many of us may have to face.

DAY 6   *Genesis 30:22-24.*
a) Rachel had, no doubt, prayed for a child for a long time. Why do you suppose God had delayed the answer?
b) What does this teach us about prayer?

QUESTIONS (contd.)

DAY 7   *Genesis 31:1-35.*

a) Which verses show us that Rachel and Leah are now united in purpose and in trust in God? (Ps. 133).

b) And which incident shows Rachel's lapse into the old ways? What should we learn from this? (Matt. 26:41)

c) What was Jacob's last loving act towards Rachel (Gen. 35:16-20)?

NOTES

RIVALRY BETWEEN TWO SISTERS

Let us take a look at the two women we are considering in our study today:

The Main Character, RACHEL – vivacious and attractive, a replica of her aunt Rebekah, whose romance had commenced at that very well.

Her Rival, LEAH – unattractive and weak-eyed, yet steady and faithful. Both loved their clever cousin Jacob, lately arrived from Canaan.

THEIR WEDDING

Jacob fell in love with Rachel the moment he set eyes on her. He hurried forward to draw water for her sheep, and actually kissed her, a cousinly kiss maybe! Rachel and Jacob's love-story is perhaps the most famous in the Bible. He served his uncle Laban for 7 whole years for her, and they seemed to him but a few days. Maybe, to Rachel, they seemed an eternity! Poor Leah, what chance did she have with her attractive young sister around?

The 7 years drew to a close. Wedding festivities were in the air. The evening came, but it was Leah, not Rachel, who was escorted heavily veiled to her bridegroom. She must have carried out her part of the deception pretty well, for Jacob knew nothing of the deceit till the morning light revealed the unattractive face of Leah! Did he at that moment remember the day when he and his mother had succeeded in tricking his old father, Isaac?

Marriage to Rachel also took place a week later, on the understanding that Jacob should serve his father-in-law a further 7 years. How he loved this beautiful girl, a love that was fully returned. And how Leah longed to feel some response from Jacob, especially since it was she who presented him with four sons while Rachel remained childless. Several years of rivalry followed, each sister trying to outdo the other in striving for Jacob's approval. At last God gave Rachel the desire of her heart, and Joseph was born, the most beloved and famous of Jacob's twelve sons.

RECONCILIATION BETWEEN THE SISTERS

Was it the birth of Joseph that brought Rachel to a place of contentment where jealousy and rivalry ceased? We have noted that Laban, like his sister Rebekah, was an expert in cunning, and after 20 years Jacob had had enough. He started on the journey to his own country, not now as a pauper but with great wealth. God had carried out His promise of Genesis 28:13-15.

The two sisters were now united in their desire to leave their father's home for the new life in Canaan. They were united in the adventures of the road, and in the fear they shared with Jacob of the coming confrontation with Esau. Together they saw that God was in control, and their faith in Him grew.

And later as Rachel travailed with her second son, we can be sure that sister Leah would be there helping, comforting Jacob, and caring for Rachel's two motherless boys along with her own.

There are aspects in the lives of these two women with which we can identify. Trials and testings come to us all. They are the material God uses to shape our characters. Accept them, trusting Jesus to supply the needed grace, and we grow into loving, understanding people. Rebel, and we become bitter, resentful people. Remember, the goldsmith must put the gold into the crucible and apply the heat in order to purify it.

KEY THOUGHT: FAITH enables us to face life's testings.

STUDY 8

ASA – TURNING FROM TOTAL TRUST
BRINGS TROUBLE

QUESTIONS

DAY 1 *2 Chronicles 14:1-11.*
a) List Asa's priorities. What were the results of establishing those priorities in the land?
b) See also chapter 15:15. Can you see a personal application of this for you. See Ephesians 6:10-18.

DAY 2 *2 Chronicles 14:11-15.*
a) Asa's army was vastly outnumbered, yet he had an astonishing victory. How do you account for this?
b) The Israeli army still had quite a task to accomplish. What was it?

DAY 3 *2 Chronicles 15:1-8.*
a) Spot the remarkable promise in this section. Compare it with other promises like Isaiah 55:6, 7; Psalm 37:3-6; James 4:6-8. What are the two parts of every Divine promise?
b) What do you feel the response should be when people moan about the troubles in the world?

DAY 4 *2 Chronicles 15:9-15.*
a) What effect did Asa's total trust have on some of the other Israelite tribes?
b) Israel 'entered into a covenant' and 'sacrificed to the Lord.' What would our modern equivalents be?

DAY 5 *1 Kings 15:9-15; 2 Chronicles 15:16-19.*
Here is an instance of allegiance to the Lord coming before family loyalty.
a) What did Jesus say about this (Matt. 10:36; Luke 14:26)?
b) Sodomites (1 Kgs. 15:12 KJV) were homosexuals. What attitude should Christians have to them (Deut. 23:17; Rom. 1:26-28)?

DAY 6 *2 Chronicles 16:1-9.*
a) Contrast Asa's conniving here, compared to his attitude when the Cushites (Ethiopians or Sudanese) attacked (ch. 14:11).
b) In what respects was Asa the loser?
c) What picture of the Lord is created by Hanani's assertion in verse 9?

DAY 7 *2 Chronicles 16:10-14.*
a) More actions spoil the picture we had earlier of Asa's total trust. What are they?
b) It is obviously not wrong to have the help of doctors. Where did Asa go wrong?

NOTES

THE BACKGROUND

The Kingdom of Israel was united under Saul; then followed David and Solomon. But in the days of King Rehoboam, Solomon's son, a rebellion against his type of rule was led by Jeroboam. This led to the division of the tribes. Judah and Benjamin stayed loyal to Rehoboam and constituted the Kingdom of Judah. The remaining ten tribes united together and became the Kingdom of Israel. The Northern Kingdom (Israel) continued for 240 years until it was overthrown by the Assyrians. The Southern Kingdom (Judah) continued for another 130 years after the end of the Northern Kingdom, and it eventually succumbed to the Babylonians.

Asa was the third king of Judah after the separation from Israel.

THE KING SETS THE PACE

The first ten years of his reign were prosperous and peaceful. Two accounts of it are given in I Kings 15:1-24 and in 2 Chronicles 14-16. His heart was set on pleasing the Lord and he took steps necessary to rid the land of idolatry. He even deposed the 'queen mother' Maacah because of her idolatrous leanings, I Kings 15:13.

THE CRUNCH

The big crisis of his reign was when Zerah the Ethiopian came to attack with a huge army, 2 Chronicles 14:9. It is at this point, when vastly outnumbered, that Asa comes through with his magnificent faith-declaration. 'Lord, there is no one like you to help the powerless against the mighty. Help us, O Lord our God, for we rely on you and in your name we have come against this vast army' (2 Chron. 14:11). A tremendous victory ensues and the Ethiopians are utterly routed. After this, Asa goes on to be the key figure in a national revival.

THE DOWNTURN

Then follows a time of peace and prosperity for over twenty years, until Baasha, king of the Northern Kingdom attacks. In this test Asa's faith crumples. Trusting in man rather than in the Lord, he makes an alliance with the heathen king Ben-hadad of Damascus, who having been well paid, attacks the north of Baasha's territory. Baasha has to leave off building his fortress at Ramah and return home. Asa uses the building materials from Ramah to build two cities for himself.

But Hanani the prophet denounces Asa's lack of trust in the Lord and his allegiance with a heathen king. Asa, offended and upset at this moment of truth, puts Hanani in prison. So, from the spiritual 'high' at the time of Zerah's invasion he descends to a spiritual 'low'.

THE WARNING OF ASA'S LIFE

As the years roll on, Asa becomes LESS faithful to the Lord rather than MORE so. What a lesson for those of us in later life! It's so easy to make excuses for being less zealous for the Lord than we were in earlier days. If we are less intense for Jesus now than we have been in the past, we are BACKSLIDERS. Let's be honest with ourselves and with God.

KEY THOUGHT: 'When faith is at its normal tension, the life of sin is inconceivable'

James Denny.

The 'muscles' of faith constantly exercised, never atrophy.

STUDY 9

JOCHEBED AND MIRIAM –
FAITH, THE CHILDREN'S HERITAGE

QUESTIONS

DAY 1 *Exodus 1.*
a) What was the decree made by the king of Egypt concerning newborn Israelite babies?
b) Why did he make such a decree?

DAY 2 *Exodus 2:1-10; 6:20; Numbers 3:5-7.*
a) What do we know about the tribe to which Amram and Jochebed belonged?
b) What do we see of Jochebed's character in the episode of this chapter?
c) Whose faith was commended in Hebrews 11:23?

DAY 3 *Read Exodus 2:1-10 again.*
a) Why was Moses now safe in the home of his parents (v. 9)?
b) How would you describe the young girl Miriam?

DAY 4 *Exodus 15:20, 21; 1 Chronicles 15:25-29; 2 Chronicles 20:19-24; Nehemiah 12:27,43; Matthew 26:30; Acts 16:25.*
a) In what various kinds of circumstances in the Bible did people sing praises to God?
b) What value is there in praising God?

DAY 5 *Numbers 12; Deuteronomy 24:9; Isaiah 53:7.*
a) On what grounds did Miriam criticize her brother Moses?
b) Did Moses vindicate himself? What happened?
c) What can we learn from this?

DAY 6 *Matthew 18:15-17, 21, 22; Galatians 6:1.*
a) What does Jesus teach us to do if we have some real grievance against a brother (or sister)?
b) What is our attitude to be towards those God has put in positions of leadership (1 Thess. 5:12, 13; Heb. 13:17)?

DAY 7 *Exodus 15:20; Numbers 20:1; 1 Chronicles 6:3; Micah 6:4.*
a) What do these references tell us of the importance of Miriam to the Israelite nation?
b) What lessons have your learned from the life of this woman?

NOTES

JOCHEBED (Exod. 2:1-10)

We can never over-emphasize the influence a woman of faith has on her children. One such woman was Jochebed, a woman of:

Initiative – she planned the brilliant strategy that saved her baby's life.
Courage – she carried it out, knowing the danger involved.
Faith – she believed God had guided and she must succeed.

THE RESULT: Her faith was rewarded. Baby Moses was saved from death to become the son of the Egyptian princess and receive an education otherwise out of his reach. God was preparing him to become the leader, who would bring His nation out of slavery. God was in control and enabled Jochebed to care for her child during his early formative years. And we can be sure her prayers kept his faith strong during the 40 years spent in the heathen atmosphere of the palace. Through the godly influence of Jochebed and her husband, their other two children Aaron and Miriam also became leaders in their nation.

MIRIAM

We have 3 incidents recorded that give us a picture of this woman:

1. *As a 7 year old girl – Exodus 2.* A small girl paddling in the Nile would arouse less suspicion than the baby's mother loitering nearby. She played her part admirably as she approached the princess and offered to find a nurse for baby Moses. We see in Miriam a child of unusual intelligence and poise, and we share her joy as she sees her little brother again being cared for in her own home. Surely, this incident strengthened young Miriam's faith in a living, loving God.

2. *As an 87 year old woman – Exodus 15:20, 21.* As Miriam witnessed the miracle of 2 million Israelites escaping through the Red Sea, her joy knew no bounds. Old Miriam grabs a tambourine and leads the women in a song and dance of praise. It did not worry her that her steps were not as graceful as in her youth, or that her voice might be getting just a little croaky. We, too, are never too old (or young) to express joyful praise. And faith expressed in praise is always contagious.

3. *As a Still Older Woman – Numbers 12.* Sad though this incident is, the Bible always 'tells it as it is'. Miriam became jealous of her brother Moses' leadership. Was she not a prophetess? And was not brother Aaron the High Priest? So she started a 'whispering campaign' against Moses for marrying a foreign wife. Aaron joined in, and the gossip was spreading. God had to make an example of her. Miriam was stricken with leprosy for 7 days, and had to remain outside the camp. Severe? God had to teach her (and us) how damaging a critical tongue can be, especially when directed against those He has placed in leadership.

Apart from this one unfortunate incident, we see in Miriam a woman of faith with leadership abilities. Most women of the Bible are recorded as the wife of some famous man. Miriam apparently remained single, yet found complete fulfilment in the service of God. Many women

FOCUS ON FAITH • STUDY 9 • JOCHEBED AND MIRIAM

experience the same today. In Micah 6:4 she is named alongside Moses and Aaron, as the ones God raised up to redeem His people. And in I Chronicles 6:3 among the list of 'the sons of ...' we read, 'the children of Amram: Aaron, Moses and Miriam.' Surely their parents were largely responsible for producing such children of faith.

KEY THOUGHT: Faith is the greatest heritage we can pass on to our children.

STUDY 10
HEZEKIAH – FOREMOST IN FAITH

QUESTIONS

DAY 1 *2 Kings 18:1-8.*
a) James 2:17-22 says that the evidence of true faith is action. Describe some of the practical outcomes of Hezekiah's faith.
b) What can we learn from the sequence from verse 6 to verse 7?

DAY 2 *2 Kings 18:13-22.*
a) How successful in the long run was Hezekiah's attempt to 'buy off' Sennacherib (see v. 17)?
b) The Assyrian general (i.e. Rabshakeh) implies that the visible world is the real world and that the invisible is unreal or less significant. What is your answer when you are tempted to feel the same?

DAY 3 *2 Kings 18:23-25.*
a) Summarise the Assyrian official's tactics. (Can you recognize a familiar pattern in your temptations?)
b) 'Do not let Hezekiah deceive you' (v. 29). 'Do not let Hezekiah persuade you' (v. 30). 'Do not listen to Hezekiah' (vv. 31, 32). What do you deduce from this?

DAY 4 *2 Kings 19:1-13.*
a) What was Isaiah's role in this crisis? What would he bring to the situation?
b) Can you see two levels in Hezekiah's reaction during the crisis? Is there encouragement for you in this?

DAY 5 *2 Kings 19:14-37.*
a) Are you under pressure these days? Can you learn anything from the ingredients of Hezekiah's prayer?
b) We don't have a prophet to go to for advice! But we do have ...?

DAY 6 *2 Kings 20:1-11.*
a) Did God change His mind? Or is there another explanation? See the parallel account in 2 Chronicles 32:24-26.
b) Isaiah is a key figure in this incident. What unique quality did he show?

DAY 7 a) Hezekiah takes a course of action displeasing to the Lord. What was at the root of it? See also 2 Chronicles 32:27-33.
b) God seemed willing to encourage Hezekiah with a sign (v. 8). Yet Jesus discouraged people from asking for signs (Matt. 12:38). Can you explain this?

NOTES

A TERRIBLE SITUATION
What an unpromising situation Hezekiah inherited from his father, Ahaz! He had left a weak kingdom under the threat of invasion by the Assyrians and other foreign powers. Coupled with that, the spiritual life of the people was at an all-time low. The Temple was closed. No one was interested in hearing about the Lord, (Isa. 6:10) and religion was just a perfunctory ritual (Isa. 29:13).

TOP MARKS FOR FAITH
Yet of all Judah's kings, Hezekiah gets top marks for his spiritual intensity and the vibrancy of his faith. He was not left on his own. God had His man in Isaiah (and others) who were instruments of guidance for the young king. But it was his leadership at this crucial time that God blessed in improving the lot of the common people. It was he who clearly wanted to follow the directive of the prophet, Isaiah, who relayed the message of the Lord to the nation: 'In returning and rest shall you be saved. In quietness and confidence shall be your strength' (Isa. 30:15).

TIPTOP ADMINISTRATOR
Three accounts of his reign are given: 2 Kings 18-20, 2 Chronicles 29-32, and Isaiah 36-39. Note the numerous accomplishments of his reign which were for the good of the nation:

Opening and repair of the Temple – 2 Chronicles 29:3-19.
Organization of public worship – 2 Chronicles 29:20, 30.
Termination of idolatrous practices – 2 Chronicles 31:1; 2 Kings 18:4.
Organization of and provision for the priesthood – 2 Chronicles 31.
Strengthening of Jerusalem by more defence-works – 2 Chronicles 32:1-8.
Improvement to the city's water supply – 2 Chronicles 32:4; 2 Kings 20:20.

A TEST FOR HIS TRUST
After the wobbly episode of buying off his enemy Sennacherib with a gift of 11 tons of silver and 1 ton of gold, the high point of his experience came when he later refused to bow further to Assyrian threats. He made a deliberate decision to trust God ALONE in a subsequent time of threat. The Lord, of course, blessed him for his faith and delivered him and the people. The story comes in 2 Kings 18 and 19. (See Ps. 62 for more on trusting God ALONE.)

A TOUGH QUESTION
Was Hezekiah justified in pleading with God for an extension of his life-span (Isa. 38:3)? After all, he was only 39 at the time! He started to reign at the age of 25 and reigned 29 years, including the 15-year extension which God granted him in answer to his request (2 Kgs. 18:2).
It is an interesting sidelight to note that Manasseh, Hezekiah's son, was 12 years old when he began to reign (2 Kgs. 21:1), so he must have been born within the 15-year extension which God gave (2 Kgs. 20:6). Manasseh was described as the wickedest of the kings of Judah – the exact opposite to his father (2 Kgs. 21:1-17). Israel would have been spared this terrible episode

if Hezekiah had accepted God's pattern in life and in death. Does the principle stated in Psalm 106:15 apply here? ('He gave them their request but sent leanness to their soul.')

A TREMENDOUS EVENT

The confirmatory sign that God was going to let Hezekiah live longer would have required a tremendous miracle. We may feel inclined to give it a physical explanation. (There actually WAS an eclipse in 689 BC, which would have been during his reign.) But we are STILL faced with supernatural factors such as Isaiah's knowledge of the forthcoming event and God's timing of it.

THE TROUGH OF SELF-SATISFACTION

After Hezekiah's great crisis of faith, we would imagine that he would never again waver. But we have another incident in which he takes his eyes away from the Lord and starts to glory in earthly values.

The visit of Merodach-Baladan (Isa. 39) was not just to congratulate him on getting well. He was obviously interested in some kind of alliance that would strengthen the position of both Kingdoms. Hezekiah gives him the 'full treatment' and shows him all his wealth. Isaiah is again God's messenger, but this time the word is not encouragement but condemnation.

KEY THOUGHT: Be sure to MAINTAIN faith after experiencing 'MOUNTAIN' faith. Beware of a Satanic counterattack after a spiritual 'high'.

ANSWER GUIDE

The following pages contain an Answer Guide. It is recommended that answers to the questions be attempted before turning to this guide. It is only a guide and the answers given should not be treated as exhaustive.

GUIDE TO INTRODUCTORY STUDY

As we look into the lives of these ten Old Testament characters, five men and five women, we will see::

Study			
1	Eve	–	faith introduced
2	Noah	–	faith's response and reward
3	Sarah & Hagar	–	faith blossoming
4	Caleb	–	faith consistent, confident, conquering
5	Rebekah	–	faith diminishing
6	Gideon	–	faith overcoming fear
7	Rachel & Leah	–	faith triumphing
8	Asa	–	faith forsaken brings trouble
9	Jochebed & Miriam	–	faith, the children's heritage
10	Hezekiah	–	faith predominating

Our Introductory Study gives insights into Biblical concepts of faith illustrated from Hebrews chapter 11.

In the first section, 'What is faith?' draw out ideas about ordinary situations, e.g. faith in a bus driver or pilot that he is capable, trusting a ladder to hold one, faith in a doctor, etc. Do have a large sheet of paper and felt pen ready.

When discussing the characters in Hebrews 11, encourage each person to contribute and think through what can be learned.

Suggestions:

Abel: evidencing one's devotion to God by giving that involves sacrifice.
Enoch: living in close fellowship with, and obeying the Lord.
Noah: being obediently responsive to God's direction even though others don't understand.

Abraham:	obeying God's leading, even though it means not knowing the ultimate (8-10) purpose, confident that He will achieve His purpose through us.
Abraham:	trusting God to accomplish in one's own life what seems to be impossible (11-12).
Moses:	taking one's stand in the world as a Christian, and if necessary, suffering (24-26) financial and social loss in doing so.
Moses:	continuing to go along the line of God's revealed will against impossible odds (27-29).
Joshua:	knowing God's strategy and steadfastly going ahead with it, believing that the Lord will bring His purpose to pass eventually.
Rahab:	identifying with God's children and the cause of the Kingdom of God, rather than going the way of the world.
Gideon, etc.:	engaging in spiritual warfare against the forces of Satan, and being prepared to give one's life, if necessary, in the cause.

What is your own definition of faith?

Here is a sample: 'An absolute trust and confidence in God evidenced by sensitivity to Him and by practical steps of obedience to His revealed will, even though the path is unknown, untried, is at variance with worldly values, and involves personal sacrifice.'

* * *

In the final section of the study, work out beforehand how YOU would fit the experiences of the characters into the 3 categories: e.g.

Creative faith – Noah, Abraham.
Conquering faith – Moses, Joshua, Gideon.

Finally, it will be up to you, as leader, to encourage your group members to read books that will enrich their whole understanding of the concept of faith, and enable them to be more aware of ways to put their own faith into action.

GUIDE TO STUDY 1

DAY 1 a) Joy.
b) Husband and wife belong to each other and need each other. This bond surpasses all other relationships, and should last throughout life.

DAY 2 a) She may have been more emotionally vulnerable whereas Adam may have seen things from a logical perspective. Also, it appears God had given the instructions to Adam before Eve was created, so she would have received them from Adam.
b) Jesus was also tempted in the realm of the body, mind and spirit.
c) *Body*: overeating, illicit sex, addiction to alcohol, smoking, etc.
Mind: self-will, pride in intellectual attainments, unclean thoughts and imaginations, etc.
Spirit: spiritual pride, wanting to appear spiritual, etc.

DAY 3 a) The sword of the Spirit (the Word of God), and the shield of faith.
b) Recognition of their nakedness. While their hearts were pure they had no consciousness of this.
Because of man's fallen nature, it is necessary for people to be clothed. Note that God, Himself, clothed them.

DAY 4 a) After sinning they were afraid of God and hid from Him.
b) Their offspring were born with a bent towards sin, and judgment for sin extended to all mankind.

DAY 5 a) They admitted they had eaten the fruit.
b) They each refused to accept personal responsibility, but passed the blame on to others.

DAY 6 Women still have pain in childbirth, in spite of medical help. (Note: men have also devised mechanical help to aid them in their part of the punishment!) However, since Christ has taken our punishment on the cross, women can trust in His presence and help during childbirth.

DAY 7 a) 'It's all my fault. Why did I doubt God's goodness and disobey Him? I have failed in the training of my son. Abel is dead, and God has sent Cain away from me. Oh, comfort me God', etc.
b) To trust God's ways even though we don't understand them.
To listen to no voice that casts doubt on God's truth and love.
To keep away from the source of temptation.
When we do fail and confess it we can know there is mercy.

GUIDE TO STUDY 2

DAY 1   a) Because of his relationship with the Lord – Genesis 6:9. Because of the quality of his life – Genesis 7:1.

b) He was probably ridiculed for wasting his resources on such a vast and impractical project.

DAY 2   a) It is a symbol of salvation through Christ. As Noah was saved from physical destruction by the ark, we are saved from spiritual death by faith in Christ.

b) God's judgment will finally be just as swift and all-embracing to those who are similarly heedless of eternal values.

DAY 3   a) The idea, as in 2 Kings 4, is that of being cut off from all other sources – total dependence on God alone.

b) The passage reveals His total hatred of evil.

DAY 4   a) God's care and concern for His children and His desire to make them intelligently aware of His purposes of good for them.

b) God means us to be spiritually fruitful, i.e., our lives should have an impact on others which will lead to the extension of God's Kingdom.

DAY 5   a) Christ taught his disciples to exercise spiritual authority. Note especially Matthew 28:19-20. Believers share His authority. We are a 'royal priesthood'. Mark 11:22-24 teaches us to pray with authority.

b) The life is in the blood. Hence the blood is sacred to God, Leviticus 7:10-14.

Our salvation is based on Christ's shed blood.

DAY 6   a) Verses 9, 11, 12, 13, 15, 16, 17

b) 'I will never again send a flood as a means of universal judgment on mankind.'

c) To remove the fear from Noah and his descendants that a similar catastrophe would overtake them.

DAY 7   a) No matter how far we go in God's purposes, the possibility of falling is still present.

b) Believed, obeyed, faith.

GUIDE TO STUDY 3

DAY 1
a) Ur in Chaldea (Babylonia).
b) She was used to an advanced civilization, and would face the future with trepidation, yet with courage and faith in God and in Abraham.

DAY 2
She would feel very upset and rejected. Yet she did not want his life to be put in danger. Perhaps she trusted God to preserve her purity.

DAY 3
a) She desired that Abraham should have a son, and considered it was no longer possible that she could give birth.
b) Jealousy.

DAY 4
The teaching Abraham would have given his household.
In her extremity and need she would seek God.
God appeared to her personally, calling her by her name, on two occasions, and convinced her of His love for her.

DAY 5
a) Faith is doubt overcome, and is progressive. It grows with accepting and meditating on God's Word.
b) Mary, the mother of Jesus (without a human father to the child), Elizabeth, mother of John the Baptist (in her old age).

DAY 6
a) The first laughter was amusement at the thought of having a child in her old age. The second was the laugh of delight because God had been faithful in fulfilling His promise.
b) That his descendants would inherit the land of Canaan (Israel). That they would be numerous. That his descendants would become a great and mighty nation, and in him all nations of the earth would be blessed. His descendants would possess the gates of their enemies.
Yes, though complete fulfilment is yet to come.

DAY 7
a) Because his story would be incomplete without the co-operation and faith of his wife. They grew in faith together. She was a strong-minded woman, yet loved her husband dearly.
b) In spite of mistakes, her own and his, she was loyal and faithful, and shared Abraham's strong faith in God.

FOCUS ON FAITH • ANSWER GUIDE • • • • •

43

GUIDE TO STUDY 4

DAY 1 a) To give them a VISION of God's purpose.
The Lord wants us to be able to envisage practical goals, so that we can exercise faith for their achievement.
b) They were leaders, able by their position to motivate others.

DAY 2

THE TEN	THE TWO
'The people are strong.' 13:28	'Their protection is gone, the Lord is with us.' 14:9
'The cities are fortified and very large.' 13:28	'If the Lord is pleased with us He will lead us into that land 14:8
We can't attack; they are stronger than we.' 13:31	'We should go up and take possession, for we can certainly do it.' 13:30
'We seemed like grasshoppers.' 13:33	We will swallow them up.' 14:9
Statements are NEGATIVE	Statements are POSITIVE
Problems seen as HUGE	Problems seen in PROPORTION
UNBELIEF dominates	FAITH dominates

b) The basic attitudes of the two groups were very different.

DAY 3 a) It warns us of God's hatred of complaining, disobedience and unbelief.
b) He was absolutely 'sold out' to God and His will.

DAY 4 a) Their grumbling spirit attributed an unworthy motive to God verse 27. They blamed their leaders for undermining their morale verse 28. They gave in to fear verse 29.
b) The lovingkindness of God our Heavenly Father; His positive well-meaning care and attention; His desire to guide His children.

DAY 5 a) Caleb's wholehearted devotion to the Lord.
b) Even at 85 he was vigorous, full of faith, positive in his assertions about God and His purposes, and confident that God would give him the ability to do what needed to be done (Ps. 92:14).

DAY 6 a) His thoughtfulness in giving his daughter the water supply necessary for the land.
b) Personal answers here. Possible areas: fear, self-consciousness, self-condemnation, a critical spirit, lack of prayer, an unforgiving attitude.

DAY 7 a) All twelve spies say the SAME things, yet they reported in such a way as to create fear and panic, and undermine loyalty to the leader.
b) Personal answers here. Possible traits: positive attitude, care, concern, sympathy, knowledge of the Word and ability to apply it, discernment, straightness, love, prayer life.

FOCUS ON FAITH • ANSWER GUIDE

44

GUIDE TO STUDY 5

DAY 1
a) Beautiful, strong, kind, intelligent, strong-willed.
b) Granddaughter of Nahor, Abraham's brother, and therefore, Abraham's great-niece.

DAY 2
a) The servant was obviously a godly man from her relatives' household. She could see God's Hand in answered prayer. The expensive jewellery and the servant's account of Isaac would assure her of future comfort and security. Her family approved and gave their blessing. See also verse 50.
b) Fulfilled in her many descendants, the nation of Israel, who have maintained their nationhood in spite of many enemies.

DAY 3
a) She would ask questions about her future bridegroom and his family, their manner of life, etc.
b) Joy at knowing she was accepted and loved after her long journey. They both knew that it was God who had planned their marriage. He needed her comfort after his mother's death.

DAY 4
a) They both knew the power of prayer. Isaac prayed for his wife, and God answered. Rebekah prayed, and the Lord spoke directly to her.
20 years.
b) Because each had a favourite child.
All children should be treated without partiality by both parents.
c) Probably to offset Isaac's favouritism of Esau. She kept in mind that God had told her Jacob, not Esau the firstborn, would become head of the house. We may find that one child has a more winsome, responsive, loveable nature than another.

DAY 5
She would feel humiliated and lose respect for him.

DAY 6
a) God is quite capable of bringing about His purposes without our helping Him out.
Sarah, in giving her maid Hagar to Abraham in marriage.
b) Yes, by being unwilling to await God's timing, and trying to force what we believe to be His will.

DAY 7
a) She caused much grief to Isaac and Esau, which would have worsened her relationship with them.
Her favourite son Jacob left home, and she never saw him again.
She would be a lonely guilt-ridden woman for the rest of her life.
b) *STRENGTHS*: Physical beauty and strength, intelligence, initiative and energy. In early days, faith and love.
WEAKNESSES: Determination to get her own way at any cost, leading to ruthlessness, craftiness and hate. Possessiveness, and a passion to manipulate people for her own ends.

GUIDE TO STUDY 6

DAY 1   a) Obedience brings blessing; disobedience brings Divine retribution.
b) The angel said, 'The Lord is with you.' Gideon said, 'IF the Lord is with US why has all this happened to US?' The Lord had not been with Israel because of its waywardness.

DAY 2   a) He looked at his own limitations rather than to the Lord's resources available to him.
b) The assurance of His presence and power.

DAY 3   a) Many feel that Gideon's action was a 'second best'. That if he had allowed faith to conquer fear, he could have done without signs. Probably we should refrain from asking for signs, except when we are in an extremity such as when our emotions are involved and it is hard to recognize the witness of the Spirit.
b) He had boldness and authority, and others recognized these qualities and gave him their allegiance.

DAY 4   a) It would have stretched his faith as he realized he was wholly cast on God.
b) It gave him an understanding of the thinking of the enemy, and hence, encouragement to proceed in line with God's purpose.

DAY 5   a) He reached the place of confident praise and worship (see Rom. 4:20).
b) It would have created an illusion of a vast army because normally the tasks of torch-bearing and trumpet-blowing would have been spread throughout a large company of infantry.
c) Individual answers here.

DAY 6   a) He showed concern for his men in seeking food for them (v. 5). He showed wisdom in dealing with his critics (vv. 2, 3).
b) He promised to return and take vengeance on those who would not co-operate with him AFTER he had defeated a vastly greater army.

DAY 7   a) At least partially, because he refused further ongoing leadership responsibilities (v. 23).
b) The request for material reward, and allowing the ephod (or idol) to become an object of veneration (v. 27).

GUIDE TO STUDY 7

DAY 1
a) Rebekah's to Isaac. Moses' to Zipporah.
b) He was willing to serve 7 years for her, and she was ready to wait. Then he was prepared to serve a further 7 years.
c) Suggestions: Love, trust, tolerance, faithfulness, commitment, good communication, mutual interests, acceptance, admission when in the wrong and willingness to forgive, a sense of humour and, most important, a true faith in God.

DAY 2
a) She was equally culpable with her father.
b) There would be strong resentment and probably hate.

DAY 3
a) By giving her four sons.
b) They are a trust from God. Parents are therefore responsible to God for the way they bring them up.

DAY 4
a) Giving her servant-girl to Jacob. The resulting children would be considered Rachel's.
b) Sarah.
c) Verses 6-8. The names she gave to Bilhah's children reveal her resentment. Others are affected by our refusal to forgive.

DAY 5
a) Lack of real love from her husband in spite of giving him children.
b) She had not been able to have children.
c) Feelings of inferiority, rejection, guilt. Disappointments in not obtaining possessions or opportunities we desire. Unrequited love, loneliness, grief over death of loved ones, etc. God's grace can give victory in all circumstances.

DAY 6
a) God had to work with Rachel's wrong attitudes first. Probably He wanted to make up to Leah for the love she was not receiving from her husband.
b) Sometimes God delays the answer while He prepares us to receive it. Searching of our motives, combined with faith and perseverance, brings God's answers in God's timing.

DAY 7
a) Verses 14-16.
b) Rachel stealing and hiding her father's gods.
Need of steadfastness of purpose and continual faith in Christ to keep us true.
c) Changing her son's name from 'Son of Sorrow' to 'Son of My Right Hand', and erecting an impressive pillar over her burial place.

GUIDE TO STUDY 8

DAY 1

a) *Priority 1* was the worship of the Lord and the destruction of idols (vv. 1-5).
Priority 2 was a good defence system (vv. 6, 7).
Priority 3 was a well-equipped army (v. 8).
The Lord gave rest and peace.

b) The same will apply to us all when we:
   i. get rid of things that take precedence over our devotion to the Lord (Matt. 6:33).
   ii. build up our spiritual defence by regular devotional times (Ps. 91).
   iii. learn how to use our spiritual weapons (Eph. 6:13-18).

DAY 2

a) The power of the Lord was released because of Asa's declared TOTAL TRUST in Him, and not in his own resources.
   i. they carried off a huge amount of plunder.
   ii. they plundered and destroyed the villages around Gerar.
   iii. they attacked the herdsmen's camps and carried off livestock.

b) The lesson is that we rely wholly on the Lord, but we have to actively press our spiritual advantage to the maximum.
'Prayer is warfare. Service is picking up the spoils.'

DAY 3

a) The promise is in verse 2. In every promise there is:
   i. a condition for man to fulfil.
   ii. a commitment from God that He will act.

b) The Christian answer is that human nature, apart from the grace of God, is selfish to the point of the destruction of others. The existence of Satan and evil spirits means unending conflict. The devil manipulates the minds and desires of man who resists the control of God, Psalm 2.

DAY 4

a) Several of them abandoned idolatrous practices and came over to worship God.

b) Committing our lives to a discipleship lifestyle (Luke 14:27). Cultivating a daily devotional time of fellowship with God.

DAY 5

a) Jesus warned that the Gospel would create division even among closely related people, because each person has to make an individual decision regarding faith in Christ.

b) We should condemn the practice (as the Bible does – see Rom. 1), yet pity those ensnared in it and lovingly seek to win them to Christ, who will be the key to their release.

DAY 6   *CUSHITE CRISIS*
Relied wholly on God, declared his total trust, exterminated the enemy.
BAASHA CRISIS
Bought Ben-hadad's help, emptied the treasury, didn't finally deal with the enemy.
b) Had war from then on. Lost out in his relationship with the servant of the Lord.
c) God is constantly taking the initiative in His desire to prove His power in the lives of men and women who will trust Him wholly.

DAY 7   a) i.   Anger with God's servant and the truth he declared (v. 10).
      ii.   Vengeful action in imprisoning him and oppressing others (v. 10).
      iii. Failure to seek God in his illness (v. 12).
b) His faith was wholly and completely in the doctors, and he ignored the ultimate source of all health and goodness – the Lord.

GUIDE TO STUDY 9

DAY 1

a) Pharoah commanded the Israelite midwives that newborn male babies were to be killed. Then he commanded all his people (Egyptians) that they were to throw all newborn Israelite baby boys in the river Nile.

b) He did not remember all that Joseph had done for the Egyptian nation. He was afraid the Israelite men would fight against him in war.

DAY 2

a) The tribe of Levi was chosen by God to be the priestly tribe.

b) We see a woman of initiative, courage, intelligence and faith.

c) The parents' faith. Amram would have been in agreement with Jochebed's scheme.

DAY 3

a) Because he was now the son of the Egyptian princess.

b) Much as her mother, a girl with confidence, intelligence, poise and courage.

DAY 4

a) In celebrating victory in war, in dedications, in religious festivals, in showing faith when facing enemies and when facing sorrow and trials.

b) Praise glorifies and pleases God. It takes our eyes off our problems and sets them on God who solves them. It brings victory over fears, worry, depression, changing them into joy and faith. It defeats Satan.

DAY 5

a) On the grounds that he married a foreign wife, though the real motive was jealousy of his leadership.

b) No, God vindicated him.

c) That we can trust God to vindicate us when wrongly criticized.

DAY 6

a) To forgive him (her). However, if the fault is sufficiently serious, we should talk it over with him alone, then take one or two witnesses, and as a last resort bring it to the Church. The motive should be to restore, not condemn.

b) To esteem them very highly in love.

DAY 7

a) Miriam is mentioned alongside Moses and Aaron in the genealogies of Israel, and as one of the leaders through whom God redeemed His people from slavery. The place of her death and burial are recorded, which signify her importance to the nation. She is known as a prophetess.

b) God chooses and equips women for positions of leadership. Though He uses our natural endowments, He is more concerned to develop humility and faith as qualifications for spiritual leadership. Even godly people fail, but God is willing to forgive and continue to use them.

GUIDE TO STUDY 10

DAY 1
a) He did everything he could to abolish idolatry; He sought to follow the code God gave Moses; He shook off the domination of a heathen power (Assyria); He defeated the perennial enemy – the Philistines.
b) The obedient life brings the blessing of the Lord (See also v. 12, which relates to the northern Kingdom, Samaria).

DAY 2
a) It only delayed the day of reckoning.
b) The more vital our prayer life and the closer our walk with the Lord, the easier it is to withstand suggestions that the invisible world is unreal or less significant.

DAY 3
a) Mockery, plus insinuations of total weakness and inability to cope; Assertion that he had an authentic message from the Lord; Sought to undermine confidence in leadership; Assertion of the lie that he was in complete control.
b) The strength of Judah lay in Hezekiah's integrity and spirituality, hence he is Rabshakeh's main target.

DAY 4
a) Spiritual adviser.
Because of his prophetic gift and close walk with the Lord he was able to encourage the king and bring a word from the Lord that put his mind at rest. (Do you have a good spiritual counsellor? Could you help someone else by being a counsellor?).
b) *Level 1*: a perfectly normal human reaction of anxiety and fear, (v. 1).
Level 2: recourse to the Lord in faith and expectancy (vv. 2-6).

DAY 5
a) The basic ingredients of Hezekiah's prayer were: He took time to go to the place of prayer; He spread the matter in detail before the Lord; He waited on the Lord and opened his heart to the Lord; He pleaded for deliverance; He asserted that such a deliverance would glorify God among the nations.
b) The Word of God, the Holy Spirit, and (probably) sympathetic Christian fellowship and wise spiritual counsellors.

DAY 6
a) The 2 Chronicles version indicated that there was a measure of ultimate repentance on Hezekiah's part and for this reason God spared him.
b) Sensitivity, in that he immediately responded to the changed instructions from the Lord.

DAY 7
a) He made a proud display of his possessions without any indication of giving the glory to the Lord. Note the comment in 2 Chronicles 32:31 that 'God left him to test what was in his heart.'
b) Hezekiah was a follower of the Lord. The people to whom Jesus referred were worldlings whose hearts were set against Him. However, God is our loving Heavenly Father and frequently gives outward indications to guide and encourage us.

THE WORD WORLDWIDE

We first heard of WORD WORLDWIDE over 20 years ago when Marie Dinnen, its founder, shared excitedly about the wonderful way ministry to one needy woman had exploded to touch many lives. It was great to see the Word of God being made central in the lives of thousands of men and women, then to witness the life-changing results of them applying the Word to their circumstances. Over the years the vision for WORD WORLDWIDE has not dimmed in the hearts of those who are involved in this ministry. God is still at work through His Word and in today's self-seeking society, the Word is even more relevant to those who desire true meaning and purpose in life. WORD WORLDWIDE is a ministry of WEC International, an interdenominational missionary society, whose sole purpose is to see Christ known, loved and worshipped by all, particularly those who have yet to hear of His wonderful name. This ministry is a vital part of our work and we warmly recommend the WORD WORLDWIDE 'Geared for Growth' Bible studies to you. We know that as you study His Word you will be enriched in your personal walk with Christ. It is our hope that as you are blessed through these studies, you will find opportunities to help others discover a personal relationship with Jesus. As a mission we would encourage you to work with us to make Christ known to the ends of the earth.

Stewart and Jean Moulds – British Directors, **WEC International.**

OLD TESTAMENT

1-85792 885 7
Messenger of Love
A study in Malachi

1-85792-888-1
Triumph over Failures
A study in Judges

0-90806-755-0
A Saviour is Promised
A study in Isaiah 1-39
John Priddle

0-90806-706-2
Hypocrisy in Religion
A study in Amos
Marie Dinnen

0-90806-728-3
The Beginning of Everything
A study in Genesis 1-11
Marie Dinnen

0-90806-751-8
Unshakeable Confidence
A study in Habakkuk and Joel
A. Bakes

THEMES

1-85792-892-X
God's Heart, My Heart
What the Bible Says about World
Mission

0-90806-739-9
Finding Christ in the Old Testament
A Study in Pre-existence and
Prophecy
Dorothy Russell

0-90806-720-8
Freely Forgiven
A study on Redemption
Marie Dinnen

0-90806-702-X
Freedom You Can Find It!
Marie Dinnen

0-90082-880-3
Understanding the Way of Salvation
Carol Jones

FOCUS ON FAITH . . . . .

53

CHARACTERS

1-85792-887-3
Abraham-A study in Genesis
A Study in Genesis 12-25

1-85792-889-X
Serving the Lord
A study in Joshua

1-85792-890-3
Focus on Faith
A Study of 10 OT Characters

0-90806-761-5
The Cost of Obedience
A Study of Jeremiah
Dorothy Russell

0-90806-746-1
A Man After God's Own Heart
A study of David
Esma Cardinal

0-90806-700-3
God Plans for Good
A study of Joseph
Dorothy Russell

0-90806-707-0
Achieving the Impossible
A study of Nehemiah
Dorothy Russell

NEW TESTAMENT

1-85792-886-5
The Worlds Only Hope
A study in Luke

1-85792-891-1
Walking in Love
A Study in John's Epistles

0-90806-736 4
The Early Church
A study in Acts 1-12
Esma Cardinal

0-90806-7216
Made Completely New
A Study in Colossians and
Philemon
Dorothy Russell

0-90806-716-X
Jesus-who is he?
A Study in John's Gospel

0-90806-701-1
Faith That Works
A study in James
Marie Dinnen

A full list of over 50 'Geared for Growth' studies can be obtained from:

ENGLAND   *North East/South*: John and Ann Edwards
5 Louvaine Terrace, Hetton-le-Hole, Tyne & Wear, DH5 9PP
Tel. 0191 5262803 Email: rhysjohn.edwards@virgin.net
North West/Midlands: Anne Jenkins
2 Windermere Road, Carnforth, Lancs., LA5 9AR
Tel. 01524 734797 Email: anne@jenkins.abelgratis.com
West: Pam Riches Tel. 01594 834241

IRELAND   Steffney Preston
33 Harcourts Hill, Portadown, Craigavon, N. Ireland, BT62 3RE
Tel. 028 3833 7844 Email: sa.preston@talk21.com

SCOTLAND Margaret Halliday
10 Douglas Drive, Newton Mearns, Glasgow, G77 6HR
Tel. 0141 639 8695 Email: mhalliday@onetel.net.uk

WALES   William and Eirian Edwards
Penlan Uchaf, Carmarthen Road, Kidwelly, Carms., SA17 5AF
Tel. 01554 890423 Email: penlanuchaf@fwi.co.uk

UK CO-ORDINATOR
Anne Jenkins
2 Windermere Road, Carnforth, Lancs., LA5 9AR
Tel. 01524 734797 Email: anne@jenkins.abelgratis.com

UK Website: www.wordworldwide.org.uk